To Jewish librarians—keepers of the flame
And to Jennifer, whose big idea was to convert to Judaism
and teach me about my own heritage—R.M.

In loving memory of my grandfather, Dr. Irving Koffler,
who always supported the family's artistic endeavors—A.R.

Rocky Pond Books
An imprint of Penguin Random House LLC
1745 Broadway, New York, New York 10019

First published in the United States of America by Rocky Pond Books, an imprint of Penguin Random House LLC, 2025

Text copyright © 2025 by Richard Michelson

Illustrations copyright © 2025 by Alyssa Russell

Visit us online at PenguinRandomHouse.com.

Library of Congress Cataloging-in-Publication Data is available.

ISBN 9798217003259

Manufactured in China · TOPL · 10 9 8 7 6 5 4 3 2 1

Design by Cerise Steel · Text set in FS Rosa

The artist created the illustrations in this book using an iPad and Procreate along with period-specific research.

The author would especially like to thank: Phyllis Erlichman for trusting me with her aunt's story; and Naomi Firestone-Teeter for her unflagging encouragement, and for shepherding the Jewish Book Council into the next hundred years. Fanny would be thrilled to see how her big idea has been nurtured and grown. Thanks as well to Chris Barash, Sylvia Glick, Joy Kingsolver, Kate Larson, Eve Neiger, Jonathan Sarna, Andrea Rapp, Rabbi Ben Weiner, and Carolyn Yoder. It takes a village to write a book and each of you offered encouragement, shared information, or helped point me in the right direction. Finally, I give thanks to my amazing editor, Lauri Hornik, for making this book happen in time for the 100th anniversary of the Jewish Book Council. I didn't think it would be possible.—R.M.

The authorized representative in the EU for product safety and compliance is Penguin Random House Ireland,
Morrison Chambers, 32 Nassau Street, Dublin D02 YH68, Ireland, https://eu-contact.penguin.ie.

FANNY'S BIG IDEA

How Jewish Book Week Was Born

written by **Richard Michelson**

illustrated by **Alyssa Russell**

Rocky Pond Books

Fanny loved the busyness of her new neighborhood in Boston's North End. Almost all her friends were immigrants, and everybody had their own traditions. But some days Fanny missed her books, her dolls, and the fancy dresses she had to leave behind.

She was born in Russia, where her parents were leaders of the Jewish community. "My bubbe even met the Emperor, Tzar Nicholas the Second," Fanny told her new neighbors. "She brought him books about Jewish customs.

"But the tzar didn't want to read about people different from himself. He told the police to burn down our house if we went to synagogue instead of church."

Fanny was six years old when she came to America with her big sister, Esther, and her little brother, Henry. Her parents wanted a safe place to practice their religion. They carried only their silver samovar to remind them of home.

The giant teapot almost filled
the entire kitchen in the tiny
apartment they rented in a
tenement filled with refugees.

Once a week Fanny walked to the North End Settlement House, a school that taught immigrants about American customs. She was excited to study English, and to learn about Thanksgiving and the Fourth of July.

Some of her teachers were students from nearby Harvard University and Simmons College. After class, Fanny tried to teach them Yiddish, and explain the difference between Sukkot and Shavuot. But they didn't seem interested in learning different traditions. You need to be "more American," they told Fanny.

And you need to dress "more ladylike," a wealthy society woman added. She had stopped by to teach the girls "proper manners." She frowned when she saw Fanny's threadbare clothes and offered to buy her a pretty outfit.

"I once had a closet of fancy dresses," Fanny replied. "In this country Papa is a poor peddler, but I am the same person no matter what I wear."

What mattered to Fanny was that in America, you could read books for free. She visited the Settlement House library every day and was proud to hear Papa call her "my little rabbi" because she was always studying.

Fanny didn't think it was fair that she couldn't attend a yeshiva, the schools where boys learned about the Torah and other Jewish religious texts, but she loved lighting the Sabbath candles with Mama and chanting the traditional blessings.

Fanny was excited to graduate from Hancock Grammar. That was more schooling than most girls in the neighborhood, and she hoped to go to high school and maybe even college to become a doctor.

But an infection called tuberculosis spread through the tenements. Papa got a bad fever, and the next day he was taken to the hospital.

Fanny sat up all night comforting her two younger American-born sisters, Ida and Rose. She knew Papa was never coming home. It was time to find a job and help Mama.

After her father died, Fanny's neighbors offered advice.

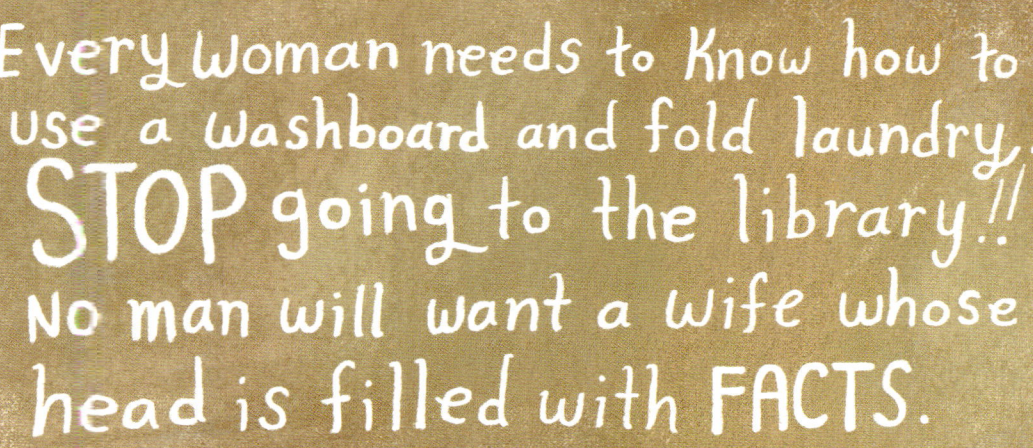

Every woman needs to know how to use a washboard and fold laundry. STOP going to the library!! No man will want a wife whose head is filled with FACTS.

"I will join a club," Fanny answered, "but I do not intend to be treated like a cat. All girls should learn to take care of themselves."

Fanny walked straight to the North Bennet Street reading room, where Miss Edith Guerrier, a librarian at the Boston Public Library, had started the Saturday Evening Girls Club to prove that immigrant girls were as smart as everyone else.

There were lectures about democracy, women's rights, and prison reform. There were dramatic readings, arts and crafts projects, folk dancing, and singing. And best of all, there was hot chocolate and cookies.

Week after week, month after month, Fanny never missed a meeting.

She appointed herself the club's "unofficial greeter," welcoming younger members. She loved hearing stories about their traditions as much as she enjoyed sharing hers. Some of the girls were Jewish, but most were Catholic or Protestant. Many were from Ireland or Italy.

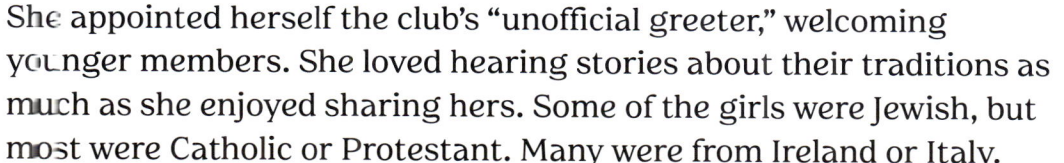

Fanny fed the library kitten and named her Beatrice Alighieri, after the Italian author Dante Alighieri.

Some days Fanny sneaked into the boys' book room to learn about inventors, presidents, and explorers. When no one was looking, she moved Stevenson's *Treasure Island* and Shakespeare's *Winter's Tale* into the girls' reading room.

"I love *Little Woman* and *Cinderella*," she told Miss Guerrier, "but why should boys get to explore while girls do the chores and the housework?"

Miss Guerrier helped Fanny move half the boys' books across the hall. The next Saturday she offered to pay Fanny to be her assistant.

Fanny started a Saturday Evening Girls newsletter and appointed herself editor in chief. She couldn't wait to save enough money to attend summer classes at Simmons College.

"I want to create a better world, not just survive in this one," she told Miss Guerrier. "When immigrants seek understanding and opportunity, they drift into the library."

New immigrants were moving into the North End. They were Armenian, Syrian, and Chinese. Fanny added books written by Armenian, Syrian, and Chinese authors. When Black families began to arrive from the South, Fanny added books by Black authors too. She learned everything she could about the library patrons, and she offered everyone who walked through the door a warm welcome.

Everyone should appreciate their neighbors' customs. I want to spread the idea that one can respect another person even though they are different.

As they grew older, many of Fanny's friends from the Saturday Evening Girls Club moved into larger homes in Boston's West End. They became shop owners, potters, and lawyers, most with husbands and children.

Fanny did not marry or have children, but she treated every library patron as part of her family.

When she was thirty-three years old, she was offered the job of Director of the West End Boston Public Library branch. She was the first Jewish person to direct a branch library.

Fanny made a list of which books had been checked out of her library most often. Sixty-seven percent were children's books. She loved *Winnie-the-Pooh*, *The Wizard of Oz*, *Rebecca of Sunnybrook Farm*, and *Heidi*. But nobody was bringing home books about their own culture.

Many children couldn't even name the country where their parents were born. Their parents had been so busy learning American customs, they had forgotten to pass down older family traditions.

Fanny had an idea.

It was 1925. Hanukkah was coming. She decided to host a week-long party at her library. She would fry latkes, braise brisket, and bake noodle kugel. Friends would bring sufganiyot, hot chocolate, and cookies.

Fanny wrote to the Boston and Jewish newspapers and announced her celebration. She invited all the Saturday Evening Girls. Miss Guerrier invited the city's art lovers, doctors, poets, and "all who love the humanities."

Fanny set up a menorah and hung signs in English and Yiddish. She even decorated a Christmas tree so that her non-Jewish patrons would feel welcome.

She made a display of books by Jewish authors. It was the first collection of Jewish books to be exhibited in a public library in the United States.

She wrote to libraries and synagogues across the country and urged them all to make similar displays.

Libraries can be...
a dispenser of peace...
The book is an aid to goodwill
...and universal brotherhood.

Fanny encouraged her many friends to help persuade their friends—whether they were Jewish or not—to spend the next seven days reading books about Jewish history, culture, and religion.

The more you know about someone's life, the harder it is not to like them.

The very first Jewish Book Week had begun.

MORE ABOUT FANNY AND JEWISH BOOK WEEK

In 1933 the *Boston Globe* reported that Fanny's exhibits about all the nationalities represented in the West End made her library "eagerly sought by hundreds [trying to find an] understanding between the cultures of the old and new worlds."

Fanny's fame as a librarian and public speaker began to spread. More and more people wanted to hear her opinions about books and the ways America was changing, but she continued to expand the spotlight with her usual wit. If she found herself the only woman on a "panel of experts," she would respond to the offer by suggesting, "Since modesty forbids me to dominate the feminine arena, what do you think about also inviting the following ladies?" She always had a list of women authors, critics, and librarians to share.

If she were asked to give a speech or to write a critical essay, she insisted the pay be equal to that offered men. If women writers were ignored in various year-end reviews, she would be the first to speak out. "Has it never occurred to you gentlemen that in a land where women are taking a vital part in the war effort, that they might be included in the Annual? I merely call this omission to your attention."

Climbing the ladder of the Public Library system, Fanny faced both sexism and antisemitism head-on. "As a Jewess you have to compete not only 50-50, but a little more. I use the feminine gender because library work is definitely carried on by women. There are very few men in the profession—unless they are in executive positions at the very top—and certainly very few Jewish men."

During the 1930s, Nazis began burning Jewish books in Germany, and Fanny spoke out with even more urgency about the necessity for books of all cultures to be available.

Throughout her career she also regularly visited local prisons to teach inmates about Jewish customs. She conducted Passover Seders behind bars and sent prisoners books.

Fanny retired from the West End Library in 1958. She died on December 26, 1961. She never married and she had no children, but she helped to raise generations of devoted book lovers.

JEWISH BOOK WEEK continued to grow each year, as more libraries around the country made their own displays and book lists. The National Committee of Jewish Book Week was founded in 1940, with Fanny as chairperson; three years later, the Jewish Book Council was formed, and they expanded Fanny's vision into Jewish Book Month, naming her honorary president. The National Jewish Book Awards were established in 1950, and the Jewish Book Council continues to promote interfaith understanding through Jewish books and festivals around the country. Today the Jewish Book Council has over 120 member organizations and arranges more than 1,300 programs each year.

After the success of Jewish Book Week, Fanny would go on to originate Negro History Week and Catholic Book Week. She even "pitched" a Boston Red Sox Book Week, though that never spread beyond Massachusetts.

"The children's room of our public libraries are where the foundations of a better world are being laid. We need more on race and religious discrimination and on democracy, on good-will and tolerance. We need literature which will yeild respect for all heritage and cultures."

— *Fanny Goldstein*

BIBLIOGRAPHY

The dialogue in this story is taken from Fanny's letters, articles, speeches, and her Saturday Evening Girls' Newsletter editorials, though I have taken the liberty of condensing and rearranging phrases to better accommodate the contemporary ear.

The on-line biographical information on Fanny Goldstein and her family is scant and often incorrect, but through sleuthing, research, and the following sources, I was able to re-create the timeline and particulars of Fanny's life.

Zoom interviews and emails with Phyllis Erlichman, Sylvia Glick, Joy Kingsolver and Kate Clifford-Larson July through November 2023

Glick, Sylvia. *With all Due Modesty: Selected Letters of Fanny Goldstein* (unpublished dissertation)

Goldstein, Fanny. "The Jewish Child in Book and: A Selected Bibliography of Juveniles for the Jewish Child's Own Bookshelf," *Jewish Book Annual*, vol. 5 (1946–1947)

Guerrier, Edith, *An independent woman: The autobiography of Edith Guerrier*, edited by Molly Matson (U of MA Press, 1992)

Larson, Kate Clifford, "The Saturday Evening Girls: A Progressive Era Library Club And The Intellectual Life Of Working Class And Immigrant Girls In Turn-Of-The-Century Boston" (*Literary Quarterly*, Volume 71 #2, University of Chicago Press, 2001)

Sarna, Jonathan D, Ellen Smith, Scott-Martin Kosofsky, *The Jews of Boston*, (Yale, 2005)

Saturday Evening Girls' Newsletters, 1912–1919

Fanny's papers are housed at the American Jewish Archives, Cincinnati, Ohio and the Boston Public Library.

Glick, Sylvia, "Fanny Goldstein and the Gospel of the Jewish Book" https://www.jewishbookcouncil.org/pb-daily/fanny-goldstein-and-the-gospel-of-the-jewish-book

Kent, Jessica A., "The Librarian of the West End: Fanny Goldstein" (Literary Boston, 2019) https://www.bostonbookblog.com/history/the-librarian-of-the-west-end

Norden, Margaret Kanof, "Necrology: Fanny Goldstein" https://www.jstor.org/stable/23874352?read-now=1&typeAccessWorkflow=login&seq=2#page_scan_tab_contents

Stern, Linda, Boston Women's Heritage Trail https://bwht.org/fanny-goldstein/

Tomasi, Adam. West End Museum—Fanny Goldstein https://thewestendmuseum.org/history/era/immigrant-neighborhood/fanny-goldstein/